**This book is to be returned on or before
the last date stamped below.**

EVERY MAN WILL SHOUT

EVERY MAN WILL SHOUT

an anthology of modern verse

Compiled by
ROGER MANSFIELD

Edited by
ISOBEL ARMSTRONG

OXFORD UNIVERSITY PRESS

Oxford University Press, Walton Street, Oxford OX2 6DP
London Glasgow New York Toronto
Delhi Bombay Calcutta Madras Karachi
Kuala Lumpur Singapore Hong Kong Tokyo
Nairobi Dar es Salaam Cape Town
Melbourne Auckland
and associates in
Beirut Berlin Ibadan Mexico City Nicosia

© *Oxford University Press 1964*

First published 1964
Reprinted 1966 (twice), 1968, 1970, 1971, 1972, 1974, 1980,
1981, 1983

Printed in Great Britain
at the University Press, Oxford
by Eric Buckley,
Printer to the University

Introduction

Many of the poems in this collection deal with personal and intense experiences. Though these are not, of course, confined to adolescence, they often occur very powerfully at that age, and in trying to select modern poems which will appeal to young people, we have kept this in mind. Some of the poems express the first and even awkward recognition of new feelings; some explore experience with a more reflective and subtle understanding, but whatever the kind of poem, we have always tried to choose those which are fresh and direct.

This anthology contains a number of poems written by young people still at school. We have not included these as 'curiosities', as the work of potential writers which compares with that of established poets, but rather to show what can be achieved by ordinary boys and girls who have examined their emotions and their surroundings with sensitivity and honesty.

The three sections of the anthology deal with progressively broadening themes. Similarities or sharp contrasts in mood and subject have provided the basis for our arrangement of the poems themselves.

Because this selection is primarily intended for teenagers, we have included whatever might illuminate their experience, rather than choosing a selection of representative poems by major twentieth-century poets. For the same reason we have not confined ourselves to poems by English poets, or even to poems originally written in English. All the poems by adult poets have been presented to secondary school students of varying abilities, and their reactions always formed the final criterion on which we based our selection. A number of their own poems were, in fact, written in response to these and to poems by others of their own age. We hope that some teachers will use this book in the same way, to stimulate their own pupils to write. For above all we would like it to demonstrate how much the student's own writing can give him an excitement about and an understanding of poetry.

ROGER MANSFIELD   ISOBEL ARMSTRONG

Contents

THREE

◊ Indicates authors still at school when the poem was written.

'I will make a poem some day,' said the boy,
'and every man will shout when he hears it.'

The Crock of Gold
JAMES STEPHENS

ONE

Exercise Book

Two and two four
four and four eight
eight and eight sixteen . . .
Once again! says the master
Two and two four
four and four eight
eight and eight sixteen.
But look! the lyre-bird
high on the wing
the child sees it
the child hears it
the child calls it.
Save me
play with me
bird!
So the bird alights
and plays with the child
Two and two four . . .
Once again! says the master
and the child plays
and the bird plays too . . .
Four and four eight
eight and eight sixteen

and twice sixteen makes what?
Twice sixteen makes nothing
least of all thirty-two
anyhow
and off they go.
For the child has hidden
the bird in his desk
and all the children
hear its song
and all the children
hear the music
and eight and eight in their turn
off they go
and four and four and two and two
in their turn fade away
and one and one make neither one nor two
but one by one off they go.
And the lyre-bird sings
and the child sings
and the master shouts
When you've quite finished playing the fool!
But all the children
are listening to the music
and the walls of the classroom
quietly crumble.
The windowpanes turn
once more to sand
the ink is sea
the desk is trees
the chalk is cliffs
and the quill pen
a bird again.

JACQUES PRÉVERT
translated by Paul Dehn

Schoolmaster

The window gives onto the white trees.
The master looks out of it at the trees,
for a long time, he looks for a long time
out through the window at the trees,
breaking his chalk slowly in one hand.
And it's only the rules of long division.
And he's forgotten the rules of long division.
Imagine not remembering long division!
A mistake on the blackboard, a mistake.
We watch him with a different attention
needing no one to hint to us about it,
there's more than difference in this attention.
The schoolmaster's wife has gone away,
we do not know where she has gone to,
we do not know why she has gone,
what we know is his wife has gone away.

His clothes are neither new nor in the fashion;
wearing the suit which he always wears
and which is neither new nor in the fashion
the master goes downstairs to the cloakroom.
He fumbles in his pocket for a ticket.
'What's the matter? Where is that ticket?
Perhaps I never picked up my ticket.
Where is the thing?' Rubbing his forehead.
'Oh, here it is. I'm getting old.
Don't argue auntie dear, I'm getting old.
You can't do much about getting old.'
We hear the door below creaking behind him.

The window gives onto the white trees.
The trees there are high and wonderful,
but they are not why we are looking out.
We look in silence at the schoolmaster.

13

He has a bent back and clumsy walk,
he moves without defences, clumsily,
worn out I ought to have said, clumsily.
Snow falling on him softly through the silence
turns him to white under the white trees.
He whitens into white like the trees.
A little longer will make him so white
we shall not see him in the whitened trees.

YEVGENY YEVTUSHENKO
*translated by Robin Milner-Gulland
and Peter Levi, S.J.*

Our Father

She said my father had whiskers and looked like God;
that he swore like a fettler, drank like a bottle;
used to run away from mother, left money for food;
called us by numbers; had a belt with a buckle.

On Sunday was churchday. We children walked behind.
He'd wear a stiff collar. He'd say good-morning.
And we made jokes about him, we were afraid
because already we understood about hating.

When we'd left the church that was so nice and still,
the minister would let us give the bells a telling—
four dong-dells; and we'd decide that Nell's
was to be the end of the world; it was time for going.

When we got home he'd take off his collar, and his shoes;
and his Sunday-special braces; and we'd whisper,
he's not like God. So that he'd belt us for the noise,
and we'd yell. And on Mondays he'd run away from mother.

RAY MATHEW

14

Saturdays

On Saturdays I play with my brother,
A cheerful little chap.
So gaily he plays digging away,
Tries to get the tadpoles in the Oxo tin,
Pokes the dog's eyes and pulls his tail.

He gets in the coke and his face gets black;
He goes in the barn and tries to ride the bike;
He picks the flowers and squashes them in his hand;
And watches the bumble bees getting the honey.

SHERON FREER

Encounter

She sat every Sunday, on the corner,
looking down the hill.
Once my young brother approached her
and she spoke to him.
She said she was Irish
but had come, before the War, to England
leaving her relations behind.
She spoke vaguely of them,
of her family's haemophilia.
He nodded, smiled, and agreed.

NOEL LEVERE

My Last Afternoon with Uncle Devereux Winslow

(1922: the stone porch of my Grandfather's summer house)

1

'I won't go with you. I want to stay with Grandpa!'
That's how I threw cold water
on my Mother and Father's
watery martini pipe dreams at Sunday dinner.
. . . Fontainebleau, Mattapoisett, Puget Sound . . .
Nowhere was anywhere after a summer
at my Grandfather's farm.
Diamond-pointed, athirst and Norman,
its alley of poplars
paraded from Grandmother's rose garden
to a scarey stand of virgin pine,
scrub, and paths forever pioneering.

One afternoon in 1922,
I sat on the stone porch, looking through
screens as black-grained as drifting coal.
Tockytock, tockytock
clumped our Alpine, Edwardian cuckoo clock,
slung with strangled, wooden game.
Our farmer was cementing a root-house under the hill.
One of my hands was cool on a pile
of black earth, the other warm
on a pile of lime. All about me
were the works of my Grandfather's hands:
snapshots of his *Liberty Bell* silver mine,
his high school at *Stukkert am Neckar,*
stogie-brown beams, fool's gold nuggets,
octagonal red tiles,
sweaty with a secret dank, crummy with ant-stale,
a Rocky Mountain chaise longue,

its legs, shellacked saplings.
A pastel-pale Huckleberry Finn
fished with a broom straw in a basin
hollowed out of millstone.
Like my Grandfather, the décor
was manly, comfortable,
overbearing, disproportioned.

What were those sunflowers? Pumpkins floating shoulder-high?
It was the sunset on Sadie and Nellie
bearing pitchers of ice-tea,
oranges, lemons, mint, and peppermints,
and the jug of shandygaff,
which Grandpa made by blending half and half
yeasty, wheezing homemade sarsaparilla with beer.
The farm, entitled *Char-de-sa*
in the Social Register,
was named for my Grandfather's children:
Charlotte, Devereux, and Sarah.
No one had died there in my lifetime . . .
Only Cinder, our Scottie puppy
paralysed from gobbling toads.
I sat mixing black earth and lime.

ROBERT LOWELL

Night Clouds

The white mares of the moon rush along the sky
Beating their golden hoofs upon the glass Heavens;
The white mares of the moon are all standing on their hind legs
Pawing at the green porcelain doors of the remote Heavens.
Fly, Mares!
Strain your utmost,
Scatter the milky dust of stars,
Or the tiger sun will leap upon you and destroy you
With one lick of his vermilion tongue.

AMY LOWELL

The Bird Escaped

Unsuspecting hopping gaily
questing beak digging deeply
Plumage iridescent gleaming
Yellow eye beholding gladly
Tasty morsels indiscriminately
Cast in long green grass.

Crouching green slit-eyed and feline
Calculating muscle
Pulsed unbreathing inching
Forward cruelty delineated
in jungle dense
moving slowly tail twitching.

Suddenly a leap and cry
of alarm as cat arches
forward in fury. Claws
Unsheathed. Too late. The
bird has risen skyward
with ruffled wing and
dragging tail.

ANN PRESTON

Hawk Roosting

I sit in the top of the wood, my eyes closed.
Inaction, no falsifying dream
Between my hooked head and my hooked feet:
Or in sleep rehearse perfect kills and eat.

The convenience of the high trees!
The air's buoyancy and the sun's ray
Are of advantage to me;
And the earth's face upward for my inspection.

18

My feet are locked upon the rough bark.
It took the whole of Creation
To produce my foot, my each feather:
Now I hold Creation in my foot

Or fly up, and revolve it all slowly—
I kill where I please because it is all mine.
There is no sophistry in my body:
My manners are tearing off heads—

The allotment of death.
For the one path of my flight is direct
Through the bones of the living.
No arguments assert my right:

The sun is behind me.
Nothing has changed since I began.
My eye has permitted no change.
I am going to keep things like this.

TED HUGHES

The Goldfish

Lazily through the clear
Shallow and deep,
He oars his chartless way,
Half-asleep,
The little paradox—so bright—so cold
Although his flesh seem formed of fire and gold.

High emperor of his dim
Bubble-empearled
Jet-shadowed greenish-shallowed
Water-world—
Like a live torch, a brand of burning gold,
He sets the wave afire and still is cold.

AUDREY ALEXANDRA BROWN

In the Snake Park

A white-hot midday in the Snake Park.
Lethargy lay here and there in coils,
And here and there a neat obsidian head
Lay dreaming on a plaited yellow pillow of its own
Loops like a pretzel or a true-love-knot.

A giant Python seemed a heap of tyres;
Two Nielsen's Vipers looked for a way out,
Sick of their cage and one another's curves;
And the long Ringsnake brought from Lembuland
Poured slowly through an opening like smoke.

Leaning intently forward a young girl
Discerned in stagnant water on a rock
A dark brown shoestring or discarded whiplash,
Then read the label to find out the name,
Then stared again: it moved. She screamed.

Old Piet Vander leant with us that day
On the low wall around the rocky space
Where amid broken quartz that cast no shade
Snakes twitched or slithered, or appeared to sleep,
Or lay invisible in the singing glare.

The sun throbbed like a fever as he spoke:
'Look carefully at this shrub with glossy leaves.'
Leaves bright as brass. 'That leaf on top
Just there, do you see that it has eyes?
That's a Green Mamba, and it's watching *you*.

'A man I once knew did survive the bite,
Saved by a doctor running with a knife,
Serum and all. He was never the same again.
Vomiting blackness, agonizing, passing blood,

Part paralysed, near gone, he felt

'(He told me later) he would burst apart;
But the worst agony was in his mind—
Unbearable nightmare, worse than total grief
Or final loss of hope, impossibly magnified
To a blind person of panic and extreme distress.'

'Why should that little head have power
To inject all horror for no reason at all?'
'Ask me another—and beware of snakes.'
The sun was like a burning-glass. Face down
The girl who screamed had fallen in a faint.

WILLIAM PLOMER

The Bear

His sullen shaggy-rimmed eyes followed my every move,
Slowly gyrating they seemed to mimic the movements of his
    massive head.
Similarly his body rolled unceasingly
From within.
As though each part possessed its own motion
And could think
And move for itself alone.
He had come forward in a lumbering, heavy spurt;
Like a beer barrel rolling down a plank.
The tremendous volume of his blood-red mouth
Yawned
So casually
But with so much menace.
And still the eye held yours.
So that you had to stay.
And then it turned.
Away.
So slowly.
Back

With that same motion
Back
To the bun-strewn
And honey-smelling back of its cage.

Welsh Incident

'But that was nothing to what things came out
From the sea-caves of Criccieth yonder.'
'What were they? Mermaids? dragons? ghosts?'
'Nothing at all of any things like that.'
'What were they, then?'

                    'All sorts of queer things,
Things never seen or heard or written about,
Very strange, un-Welsh, utterly peculiar
Things. Oh, solid enough they seemed to touch,
Had anyone dared it. Marvellous creation,
All various shapes and sizes and no sizes,
All new, each perfectly unlike his neighbour,
Though all came moving slowly out together.'
'Describe just one of them.'

                   'I am unable.'
'What were their colours?'

                   'Mostly nameless colours,
Colours you'd like to see; but one was puce
Or perhaps more like crimson, but not purplish.
Some had no colour.'

                  'Tell me, had they legs?'
'Not a leg or foot among them that I saw.'
'But did these things come out in any order?
What o'clock was it? What was the day of the week?
Who else was present? How was the weather?'
'I was coming to that. It was half-past three
On Easter Tuesday last. The sun was shining.

The Harlech Silver Band played *Marchog Jesu*
On thirty-seven shimmering instruments,
Collecting for Carnarvon's (Fever) Hospital Fund.
The populations of Pwllheli, Criccieth,
Portmadoc, Borth, Tremadoc, Penrhyndeudraeth,
Were all assembled. Criccieth's mayor addressed them
First in good Welsh and then in fluent English,
Twisting his fingers in his chain of office,
Welcoming the things. They came out on the sand,
Not keeping time to the band, moving seaward
Silently at a snail's pace. But at last
The most odd, indescribable thing of all
Which hardly one man there could see for wonder
Did something recognizably a something.'
'Well, what?'
        'It made a noise.'
                'A frightening noise?'
'No, no.'
      'A musical noise? A noise of scuffling?'
'No, but a very loud, respectable noise—
Like groaning to oneself on Sunday morning
In Chapel, close before the second psalm.'
'What did the mayor do?'
             'I was coming to that.'

                  ROBERT GRAVES

Nile Fishermen

Naked men, fishing in Nile without a licence,
kneedeep in it, pulling gaunt at stretched ropes.
Round the next bend is the police boat and the officials
ready to make an arrest on the yellow sand.

The splendid bodies are stark to the swimming sand,
taut to the ruffled water, the flickering palms,
yet swelling and quivering as they tug at the trembling ropes.
Their faces are bent along the arms and still.

Sun is torn in coloured petals on the water,
the water shivering in the heat and the north wind;
and near and far billow out white swollen crescents,
the clipping wings of felluccas, seagull sails.

A plunge in the turbid water, a quick joke stirs
a flashing of teeth, an invocation of God.
Here is food to be fetched and living from labour.
The tight ropes strain and the glittering backs for the haul.

Round the bend comes the police boat. The men scatter.
The officials blow their whistles on the golden sand.
They overtake and arrest strong bodies of men
who follow with sullen faces, and leave their nets behind.

REX WARNER

Farming

One day I went to the country
And saw a bent double farmer.
I said, 'Hallo, dear sir,' and he
Turned around with not too much glee.

He growled like a dog without a bone,
Kept tied to a chain-like lead,
Without a meal from yest'd'y noon,
'What do you want, you do-gooder?'

'I want to see an aspect of
Farming life behind the plough;

It seems quite hard yet easy to know.'
'Easy to know yet hard to learn,'
Said he. 'And he should know,' I said
To myself, 'but I won't get much
Information from a doubled-up
Farmer who's resuming his work.'

G. COURT

End of a Harvest Day

It was harvest time
and all farm hands were working
as hard as possible,
before the weather changed for the worse.
The tractor was pulling along
a hay cart.
The farm hands were loading the bales on to it.
Captain, the young sheep dog, was romping
about around the bales
and getting under everyone's feet,
getting in the way all the time.
It was a warm sunny day
and everybody was cheerful.
The work was hard
and soon all shirts were off.
The farmer's son began playing with Captain,
and his laughing and Captain's barking
echoed round the
silent hills.

The cart was almost loaded when
the young lad decided to get up
beside the tractor driver;

Captain stood by the wheel,
barking at him to come down.
But the young lad was enjoying himself
on the tractor.
He had edged his way along
the bonnet and was sitting
with his legs hanging down
over the grill at the front.
Captain must have thought
that the bonnet was big enough for two.
He jumped—
and missed.
His front legs scraped
down the side of the tractor.
Then his legs went through
the air vent.
He gave a sharp piercing yelp
and fell to the ground.

We all turned round,
to see Captain limping away.
The tractor had smashed his right front leg
and the flesh hung loose.
Except for the first yelp
he did not whimper at all.
The lad burst into tears.
And an elderly farm hand led the dog
back to the farm house.
We tried to console the boy,
but he knew as well as we did
what was going to happen.

The report was loud
and echoed for some time.
Then silence.
Although we know life is hard,
we felt a lump in our throats,

but no one admitted it.
But the day's work was finished
in silence,
without Captain's bark or the boy's laughter.

JOHN HURST

The Fear

A lantern light from deeper in the barn
Shone on a man and woman in the door
And threw their lurching shadows on a house
Nearby, all dark in every glossy window.
A horse's hoof pawed once the hollow floor,
And the back of the gig they stood beside
Moved in a little. The man grasped a wheel,
The woman spoke out sharply, 'Whoa, stand still!
I saw it just as plain as a white plate,'
She said, 'as the light on the dashboard ran
Along the bushes at the roadside—a man's face.
You *must* have seen it too.'

                              'I didn't see it.

Are you sure—'

            'Yes, I'm sure!'

                        '—it was a face?'

'Joel, I'll have to look. I can't go in,
I can't, and leave a thing like that unsettled.
Doors locked and curtains drawn will make no difference.
I always have felt strange when we came home
To the dark house after so long an absence,
And the key rattled loudly into place
Seemed to warn someone to be getting out
At one door as we entered at another.
What if I'm right, and someone all the time—
Don't hold my arm!'

27

'I say it's someone passing.'

'You speak as if this were a travelled road.
You forget where we are. What is beyond
That he'd be going to or coming from
At such an hour of night, and on foot too?
What was he standing still for in the bushes?'

'It's not so very late—it's only dark.
There's more in it than you're inclined to say.
Did he look like—?'

               'He looked like anyone.
I'll never rest tonight unless I know.
Give me the lantern.'

                   'You don't want the lantern.'

She pushed past him and got it for herself.

'You're not to come,' she said. 'This is my business
If the time's come to face it, I'm the one
To put it the right way. He'd never dare—
Listen! He kicked a stone. Hear that, hear that!
He's coming towards us. Joel, go in—please.
Hark!—I don't hear him now. But please go in.'

'In the first place you can't make me believe it's—'

'It is—or someone else he's sent to watch.
And now's the time to have it out with him
While we know definitely where he is.
Let him get off and he'll be everywhere
Around us, looking out of trees and bushes
Till I sha'n't dare to set a foot outdoors.
And I can't stand it. Joel, let me go!'

'But it's nonsense to think he'd care enough.'

'You mean you couldn't understand his caring.
Oh, but you see he hadn't had enough—
Joel, I won't—I won't—I promise you.
We mustn't say hard things. You mustn't either.'

'I'll be the one, if anybody goes!
But you give him the advantage with this light.
What couldn't he do to us standing here!
And if to see was what he wanted, why,
He has seen all there was to see and gone.'

He appeared to forget to keep his hold,
But advanced with her as she crossed the grass.

'What do you want?' she cried to all the dark.
She stretched up tall to overlook the light
That hung in both hands hot against her skirt.

'There's no one; so you're wrong,' he said.

                              'There is.—
What do you want?' she cried, and then herself
Was startled when an answer really came.

'Nothing.' It came from well along the road.

She reached out a hand to Joel for support:
The smell of scorching woollen made her faint.
'What are you doing round this house at night?'

'Nothing.' A pause: there seemed no more to say.

And then the voice again: 'You seem afraid.
I saw by the way you whipped up the horse.
I'll just come forward in the lantern light
And let you see.'

                    'Yes, do.—Joel, go back!'

29

She stood her ground against the noisy steps
That came on, but her body rocked a little.

'You see,' the voice said.

                    'Oh.' She looked and looked.

'You don't see—I've a child here by the hand.
A robber wouldn't have his family with him.'

'What's a child doing at this time of night—?'

'Out walking. Every child should have the memory
Of at least one long-after-bedtime walk.
What, son?'

'Then I should think you'd try to find
Somewhere to walk—'

                    'The highway, as it happens—
We're stopping for the fortnight down at Dean's.'

'But if that's all—Joel—you realize—
You won't think anything. You understand?
You understand that we have to be careful.
This is a very, very lonely place.
Joel!' She spoke as if she couldn't turn.
The swinging lantern lengthened to the ground,
It touched, it struck, it clattered and went out.

                                        ROBERT FROST

Breathless

(Written at 21,200 feet on May 23rd)

Heart aches,
Lungs pant
The dry air
Sorry, scant.
Legs lift
And why at all?
Loose drift,
Heavy fall.
Prod the snow
Its easiest way;
A flat step
Is holiday.
Look up,
The far stone
Is many miles
Far alone.
Grind the breath
Once more and on;
Don't look up
Till journey's done.
Must look up,
Glasses are dim.
Wrench of hand
Is breathless limb.
Pause one step,
Breath swings back;
Swallow once,
Dry throat is slack.
Then on
To the far stone;
Don't look up,
Count the steps done.

One step,
One heart-beat,
Stone no nearer
Dragging feet.
Heart aches,
Lungs pant
The dry air
Sorry, scant.

WILFRID NOYCE

The Guy

Dogs break the dust
barking across the dark;
kids, shouting, crack
the air like ice,
ravaging wood or park,
log-laden, against the year's fall.

Shadowing street
waste plot, or littered yard
they pile their tall
topheavy pyres
of branches, bent and tarred
to burn against this half-remembered ghost

as some straw Guy
who every year must flare
across the night,
fêted in fires,
flame-racked, yet unaware;
lapped in child's laughter endlessly.

ROBERT L. HOLMES

32

Firework Night

The sky is filled with sparks and flames;
the children rush about,
their cries are hardly heard among
the din of bangers, jumping jacks and rockets.

Dogs howl and cats cry—
Frightened of the noise.
The sky is filled with cordite smoke.
The fire is burning high.
Flashes here and crackles there.
A rocket soars into the sky.

Among all this noise nobody hears
a small child sobbing in the shade,
a banger exploded in his hand
and only he can feel the pain.

ERIC SIMPSON

Butch Weldy

After I got religion and steadied down
They gave me a job in the canning works,
And every morning I had to fill
The tank in the yard with gasoline,
That fed the blow-fires in the sheds
To heat the soldering irons.
And I mounted a rickety ladder to do it,
Carrying buckets full of the stuff.
One morning, as I stood there pouring,
The air grew still and seemed to heave,
And I shot up as the tank exploded,
And down I came with both legs broken,
And my eyes burned crisp as a couple of eggs.

33

For someone left a blow-fire going,
And something sucked the flame in the tank.
The Circuit Judge said whoever did it
Was a fellow-servant of mine, and so
Old Rhodes' son didn't have to pay me.
And I sat on the witness stand as blind
As Jack the Fiddler, saying over and over,
'I didn't know him at all.'

EDGAR LEE MASTERS

Accident

Ahh! at last, nearly five-thirty.
Now just the long leisurely cleaning of the bacon machine
All keen, I'll grease the wheel.
One bit of odd fat and round and round like french polishing
Gently to the blade, no blood, no pain, how neat
But off again as quick as lightning.
Go to the office
Interrupt manager—sacrilege.
'O.K. son I'm a St. John's man you know'—pompous to the last.

Masses of blood now,
Still no pain—cheated.
'Sorry about the blood on your floor'—crawl to the last.
Now the reward—the shop girls
'Oh my poor dear—does it hurt?'
Wince
'Well you know'
Wince again
'Only a little'
Oh boy! great—
Perhaps a scar to talk about
Shivering with excitement.
'Come on son I'll give you a lift to the hospital.'

CHRISTOPHER CHEEK

The Casualty

Farmers in the fields, housewives behind steamed windows,
Watch the burning aircraft across the blue sky float,
As if a firefly and a spider fought,
Far above the trees, between the washing hung out.
They wait with interest for the evening news.

But already, in a brambled ditch, suddenly-smashed
Stems twitch. In the stubble a pheasant
Is craning every way in astonishment.
The hare that hops up, quizzical, hesitant,
Flattens ears and tears madly away and the wren warns.

Some, who saw fall, smoke beckons. They jostle above,
They peer down a sunbeam as if they expected there
A snake in the gloom of the brambles or a rare flower,—
See the grave of dead leaves heave suddenly, hear
It was a man fell out of the air alive,

Hear now his groans and senses groping. They rip
The slum of weeds, leaves, barbed coils; they raise
A body that as the breeze touches it glows,
Branding their hands on his bones. Now that he has
No spine, against heaped sheaves they prop him up,

Arrange his limbs in order, open his eye,
Then stand, helpless as ghosts. In a scene
Melting in the August noon, the burned man
Bulks closer greater flesh and blood than their own,
As suddenly the heart's beat shakes his body and the eye

Widens childishly. Sympathies
Fasten to the blood like flies. Here's no heart's more
Open or large than a fist clenched, and in there
Holding close complacency its most dear
Unscratchable diamond. The tears of their eyes

Too tender to let break, start to the edge
Of such horror close as mourners can,
Greedy to share all that is undergone,
Grimace, gasp, gesture of death. Till they look down
On the handkerchief at which his eye stares up.

TED HUGHES

Panorama

The church spires reach up to the sky.
A crane moves slowly round.
The rows of houses are quietly broken by
rows of trees which stand sedately in the
concrete.
Chimneys with smoke pouring out; it
never ends.
A great white building comes towering
out like a castle.
The railway stretches quickly by.
A window with marks of paint on it separates
the air, but
a fresh clean rainbow comes hovering down
from out of the clouds, and hits a small
sedate house somewhere.

RONALD CRAPPER

The Train

The lines of steel and strength, cragged,
They began to quiver,
Stretching,
Trying to free themselves.
From a long way off came the high-pitched whine.
The speck approached.
Quickly it grew,
Faster, faster.
The diesel careered past
Casting crazy and mysterious shadows
Over the rugged ground.
The smell of oil,
The feeling of heat,
Then,
Onwards to the horizon.

ALAN HINTON

The Pylons

The secret of these hills was stone, and cottages
Of that stone made,
And crumbling roads
That turned on sudden hidden villages.

Now over these small hills they have built the concrete
That trails black wire:
Pylons, those pillars
Bare like nude, giant girls that have no secret.

The valley with its gilt and evening look
And the green chestnut
Of customary root
Are mocked dry like the parched bed of a brook.

37

But far above and far as sight endures
Like whips of anger
With lightning's danger
There runs the quick perspective of the future.

This dwarfs our emerald country by its trek
So tall with prophecy:
Dreaming of cities
Where often clouds shall lean their swan-white neck.

STEPHEN SPENDER

Epitaph on a Churchyard

Blackened trees, leafless bushes,
Leaning stones and careless thrushes
That sing above a windswept path
Where leaves rustle in the aftermath
Of the sleeping twilight days before
A sleep-walking nation went to war.

Perhaps the church had a grey slate roof, watched over
By rich green conifers which shadowed the worn-down step
At the door. Maybe the bark of the trees was red
On one side, greened on the other. Probably the
Choirboys whose voices were breaking did not realize
That they would be parting quite soon for trench, ship, sky—
Where there are medals for those who do not die.

I cannot tell.

And then I suppose that everyone's shirt was white,
That the swinging gate that must have been there was white,
And that the cricketing vicar's practised hand was white
When I was carried in there to be christened—in white.

But I know
A bomb fell.
Beneath a globe of turquoise sky,
Barred with long frowning purple clouds, I
See only the wind in the green sea
Of nettles, whistling over the rubble and the
Burnt rafters. One relichened wall
Stands, only unnoticed, to fall.

ANON.

The Moonlight Tree

It is the midst of the darkness.
The moon, glittering,
Shimmers through the boughs
Of a delicate tree,
With tinsel leaves
Holding lightly to the
Tips of its whispering fingers,
Waiting deliciously
For a gasp of wind.
Silver grass creeps and
Snuggles around the trunk
Waiting to catch them.
Meanwhile the delicate
Boughs split the moon
Into a thousand
Shattered fragments.

DENNIS PITT

After Apple-picking

My long two-pointed ladder's sticking through a tree
Toward heaven still,
And there's a barrel that I didn't fill
Beside it, and there may be two or three
Apples I didn't pick upon some bough.
But I am done with apple-picking now.
Essence of winter sleep is on the night,
The scent of apples: I am drowsing off.
I cannot rub the strangeness from my sight
I got from looking through a pane of glass
I skimmed this morning from the drinking trough
And held against the world of hoary grass.
It melted, and I let it fall and break.
But I was well
Upon my way to sleep before it fell,
And I could tell
What form my dreaming was about to take.
Magnified apples appear and disappear,
Stem end and blossom end,
And every fleck of russet showing clear.
My instep arch not only keeps the ache,
It keeps the pressure of a ladder-round.
I feel the ladder sway as the boughs bend.
And I keep hearing from the cellar bin
The rumbling sound
Of load on load of apples coming in.
For I have had too much
Of apple-picking: I am overtired
Of the great harvest I myself desired.
There were ten thousand thousand fruit to touch,
Cherish in hand, lift down, and not let fall.
For all
That struck the earth,
No matter if not bruised or spiked with stubble,

Went sure to the cider-apple heap
As of no worth.
One can see what will trouble
This sleep of mine, whatever sleep it is.
Were he not gone,
The woodchuck could say whether it's like his
Long sleep, as I describe its coming on,
Or just some human sleep.

ROBERT FROST

The Plum-tree

The back-yard has a tiny plum-tree,
It shows how small a tree can be.
Yet there it is, railed round
So no one tramps it to the ground.

It's reached its full shape, low and meagre.
O yes, it wants to grow more, it's eager
For what can't be done—
It gets too little sun.

A plum-tree no hand's ever been at
To pick a plum: it strains belief.
It is a plum-tree for all that—
We know it by the leaf.

BERTOLT BRECHT
translated by Edwin Morgan

The Wild Swans at Coole

The trees are in their autumn beauty,
The woodland paths are dry,
Under the October twilight the water
Mirrors a still sky;
Upon the brimming water among the stones
Are nine-and-fifty swans.

The nineteenth autumn has come upon me
Since I first made my count;
I saw, before I had well finished,
All suddenly mount
And scatter wheeling in great broken rings
Upon their clamorous wings.

I have looked upon those brilliant creatures,
And now my heart is sore.
All's changed since I, hearing at twilight,
The first time on this shore,
The bell-beat of their wings above my head,
Trod with a lighter tread.

Unwearied still, lover by lover,
They paddle in the cold
Companionable streams or climb the air;
Their hearts have not grown old;
Passion or conquest, wander where they will,
Attend upon them still.

But now they drift on the still water,
Mysterious, beautiful;
Among what rushes will they build,
By what lake's edge or pool
Delight men's eyes when I awake some day
To find they have flown away?

W. B. YEATS

Fog

The swirling fog,
The street lamp, at the end,
The house, the dark,
The old street can;
I can see nothing,
Nothing but the yellow
Mustardy decrepit fog.
The fog is making clouds
Round my feet,
As I walk,
I walk in heaven.
My feet sound, like
Cymbals;
Walking nowhere,
I hear
Nothing!
Except my heart-beat
Beating faster,
My breath,
My feet.
What can I feel?
I feel heavenly;
The fog is closing in upon me,
But it is heavenly.   TONY JARDINE

Fog

The fog comes
on little cat feet.

It sits looking
over harbour and city
on silent haunches
and then moves on.   CARL SANDBURG

Snow Overnight

Slow, soft, and soundless the snowflakes sink down;
Now everything is slow like them: people
stumble awkwardly over slippery
patches, like flat-footed penguins.
Grass, paths, steps are smoothly sloping
in soft curves and spreading into one;
There are no longer stones, earth, plants,
but only one whiteness that hurts the eyes.
There is no sound: the world is like a
clock that has stopped, whose ticking is not
noticed until it is not there.
Slow, soft, soundless,
And lonely.

The snow entangles trees, twists their
knotty unevenness into smoothness,
Merges them with all the other white,
Save where the great red winter sun
Tinges their topmost branches with warm pink,
The snow is everywhere, enveloping the
trees with a white net,
And hanging the twigs of bushes with
snow cobwebs.
A few people shovel snow or throw snowballs,
But they are like intruders in another world,
A world slow, soft, soundless,
And lonely.

STEPHEN ROXBURGH LONGWILL

Christmas Shopping

Spending beyond their income on gifts for Christmas—
Swing doors and crowded lifts and draperied jungles—
What shall we buy for our husbands and sons
    Different from last year?

Foxes hang by their noses behind plate glass—
Scream of macaws across festoons of paper—
Only the faces on the boxes of chocolates are free
    From boredom and crowsfeet.

Sometimes a chocolate box girl escapes in the flesh,
Lightly manoeuvres the crowd, trilling with laughter;
After a couple of years her feet and brain will
    Tire like the others.

The great windows marshal their troops for assault on the purse,
Something-and-eleven the yard, hoodwinking logic,
The eleventh hour draining the gurgling pennies
    Down the conduits

Down to the sewers of money—rats and marshgas—
Bubbling in maundering music under the pavement;
Here go the hours of routine, the weight on our eyelids—
    Pennies on corpses.

While over the street in the centrally heated public
Library dwindling figures with sloping shoulders
And hands in pockets, weighted in the boots like chessmen,
    Stare at the printed

Columns of ads, the quickset road to riches,
Starting at a little and temporary but once we're
Started who knows whether we shan't continue,
    Salaries rising,

Rising like a salmon against the bullnecked river,
Bound for the spawning ground of care-free days—
Good for a fling before the golden wheels run
    Down to a standstill.

And Christ is born—the nursery glad with baubles,
Alive with light and washable paint and children's
Eyes expects as its due the accidental
    Loot of a system.

Smell of the South—oranges in silver paper,
Dates and ginger, the benison of firelight,
The blue flames dancing round the brandied raisins,
    Smiles from above them,

Hands from above them as of gods but really
These their parents, always seen from below, them-
Selves are always anxious looking across the
    Fence to the future—

Out there lies the future gathering quickly
Its black momentum; through the tubes of London
The dead wind blows the crowds like beasts in flight from
    Fire in the forest.

The little fir trees palpitate with candles
In hundreds of chattering households where the suburb
Straggles like nervous handwriting, the margin
    Blotted with smokestacks.

Further out on the coast the lighthouse moves its
Arms of light through the fog that wads our welfare,
Moves its arms like a giant Swedish drill whose
    Mind is a vacuum.

LOUIS MACNEICE

The Eve of Christmas

It was evening before the night
That Jesus turned from dark to light.

Joseph was walking round and round,
And yet he moved not on the ground.

He looked into the heavens, and saw
The pole stood silent, star on star.

He looked into the forest: there
The leaves hung dead upon the air.

He looked into the sea, and found
It frozen, and the lively fishes bound.

And in the sky, the birds that sang
Not in feathered clouds did hang.

Said Joseph: 'What is this silence all?'
An angel spoke: 'It is no thrall,

But is a sign of great delight:
The Prince of Love is born this night.'

And Joseph said: 'Where may I find
This wonder?'—'He is all mankind,

Look, he is both farthest, nearest,
Highest, lowest, of all men the dearest.'

Then Joseph moved, and found the stars
Moved with him, and the evergreen airs,

The birds went flying, and the main
Flowed with its fishes once again.

And everywhere they went they cried:
'Love lives, when all had died!'

In Excelsis Gloria!

JAMES KIRKUP

The Donkey's Christmas

Plodding on,
From inn to inn,
No room to spare,
No room but a stable bare.
We rest,
And the following morning Jesus is born.
I gaze on the wondrous sight.
The King is born,
The King in a stable.
I see great lights,
Lights that are angels.
Everyone comes to see this sight.
I carried Mary,
Holy Mary,
Last night.

ANON.

TWO

Fern Hill

Now as I was young and easy under the apple boughs
About the lilting house and happy as the grass was green,
    The night above the dingle starry,
        Time let me hail and climb
    Golden in the heydays of his eyes,
And honoured among wagons I was prince of the apple towns
And once below a time I lordly had the trees and leaves
        Trail with daisies and barley
    Down the rivers of the windfall light.

And as I was green and carefree, famous among the barns
About the happy yard and singing as the farm was home,
    In the sun that is young once only,
        Time let me play and be
    Golden in the mercy of his means,
And green and golden I was huntsman and herdsman, the calves
Sang to my horn, the foxes on the hills barked clear and cold,
        And the sabbath rang slowly
    In the pebbles of the holy streams.

All the sun long it was running, it was lovely, the hay
Fields high as the house, the tunes from the chimneys, it was air
    And playing, lovely and watery
        And fire green as grass.

And nightly under the simple stars
As I rode to sleep the owls were bearing the farm away,
All the moon long I heard, blessed among stables, the nightjars
    Flying with the ricks, and the horses
        Flashing into the dark.

And then to awake, and the farm, like a wanderer white
With the dew, come back, the cock on his shoulder: it was all
    Shining, it was Adam and maiden,
        The sky gathered again
    And the sun grew round that very day.
So it must have been after the birth of the simple light
In the first, spinning place, the spellbound horses walking warm
    Out of the whinnying green stable
        On to the fields of praise.

And honoured among foxes and pheasants by the gay house
Under the new made clouds and happy as the heart was long,
    In the sun born over and over,
        I ran my heedless ways,
    My wishes ran through the house high hay
And nothing I cared, at my blue sky trades, that time allows
In all his tuneful turning so few and such morning songs
    Before the children green and golden
        Follow him out of grace,

Nothing I cared, in the lamb white days, that time would take me
Up to the swallow thronged loft by the shadow of my hand,
    In the moon that is always rising,
        Nor that riding to sleep
    I should hear him fly with the high fields
And wake to the farm forever fled from the childless land.
Oh as I was young and easy in the mercy of his means,
        Time held me green and dying
    Though I sang in my chains like the sea.

DYLAN THOMAS

High by the Grey Bell Tower

High by the grey bell tower
Standing on the hill of yesterday,
I look
Through an alive green many-fingered wall.

Swans of stillness on the river
Echo the wind's bell-chiming voice.
I see
Children like music laughing away the day.

Nestled in the landscape of a leaf
Lives all this life, green and very bright.
I hear
Birds sensing the sunset over the singing hills.

JANET RUSSELL

The Sea

The waves like ripples
Crumple
Against withering shores.
The dying foam retreats,
into the cluster of emerald greens.
Its emotional surface broken,
By quivering breezes.
Showing its freedom,
by violent tantrums that
beat feeble shores.
Then, going back into a tranquil
mood,
Almost accepting defeat.

M. J. JOSEY

Holiday

I remember the sea
The sea
Moaning, rumbling, grumbling, roaring,
Playing like a lion on the sinking yellow sands,
Pouncing and retreating in a swell of white-green passion
And dying,
Dying.

I remember the night,
Serene above the water, pulsing deep below,
In a dark disguise of moonlight
Fluttering over silver sands and fading,
Fading into dimness far away.

I remember the sun,
The burning warmth of human flesh on silky dunes,
The gravel heat beneath two weary feet
And the scorched, parched throats,
Choking dry.

I remember the days,
The glorious journeys into the sunset,
The sea and nights and sun
The summer heat and weariness and rest
And happiness.

COROLYN J. TURNER

On the Road

Our roof was grapes and the broad hands of the vine
as we two drank in the vine-chinky shade
of harvest France;
and wherever the white road led we could not care,
it had brought us there
to the arbour built on a valley side where time,
if time any more existed, was that river
of so profound a current, it at once
both flowed and stayed.

We two. And nothing in the whole world was lacking
It is later one realizes. I forget
the exact year or what we said. But the place
for a lifetime glows with noon. There are the rustic
table and the benches set; beyond the river
forests as soft as fallen clouds, and in
our wine and eyes I remember other noons.
It is a lot to say, nothing was lacking;
river, sun and leaves, and I am making
words to say 'grapes' and 'her skin'.

BERNARD SPENCER

In the Distance

Blossom is blooming
From out a roof,
Roof is showing between the trees.
Glasshouse,
Still.
Curtains hang silent,
Windows deep.
A line is formed,
A crooked one.

53

The colour of trees,
Dull, duller.
Hedges and stones
Mystify.
Colours are varied,
Washing ahanging.
A tall slim tree
Outstanding.
Cars lying dead in the road.
Highest point a church spire
Straight, upright.
Between two chimneys a treetop peeps,
Still, silent, deep.

ANNETTE O'CONNOR

Lessons of the War

To Alan Michell

2. *Judging Distances*

Not only how far away, but the way that you say it
Is very important. Perhaps you may never get
The knack of judging a distance, but at least you know
How to report on a landscape: the central sector,
The right of arc and that, which we had last Tuesday,
    And at least you know

That maps are of time, not place, so far as the army
Happens to be concerned—the reason being,
Is one which need not delay us. Again, you know
There are three kinds of tree, three only, the fir and the poplar,
And those which have bushy tops to; and lastly
    That things only seem to be things.

A barn is not called a barn, to put it more plainly,
Or a field in the distance, where sheep may be safely grazing.
You must never be over-sure. You must say, when reporting:
At five o'clock in the central sector is a dozen
Of what appear to be animals; whatever you do,
     Don't call the bleeders *sheep*.

I am sure that's quite clear; and suppose, for the sake of example,
The one at the end, asleep, endeavours to tell us
What he sees over there to the west, and how far away,
After first having come to attention. There to the west,
On the fields of summer the sun and the shadows bestow
     Vestments of purple and gold.

The still white dwellings are like a mirage in the heat,
And under the swaying elms a man and a woman
Lie gently together. Which is, perhaps, only to say
That there is a row of houses to the left of arc,
And that under some poplars a pair of what appear to be humans
     Appear to be loving.

Well that, for an answer, is what we might rightly call
Moderately satisfactory only, the reason being,
Is that two things have been omitted, and those are important.
The human beings, now: in what direction are they,
And how far away would you say? And do not forget
     There may be dead ground in between.

There may be dead ground in between; and I may not have got
The knack of judging a distance; I will only venture
A guess that perhaps between me and the apparent lovers,
(Who, incidently, appear by now to have finished,)
At seven o'clock from the houses, is roughly a distance
     Of about one year and a half.

HENRY REED

Prisoner

The sky
the ground
the landscape too
is spinning
around
around
the same
objects once
twice
thrice
around.
The goldfish
in his trap
swims
around
the whole day
through seeking
a non-existent
destination,
the prisoner
of a vicious
circle.

PETER VARY

Horses

The long whip lingers,
Toys with the sawdust;
The horses amble
On a disc of dreams.

The drumsticks flower
In pink percussion

To mix with the metal
Petals of brass.

The needle runs
In narrower circles;
The long whip leaps
And leads them inward.

Piebald horses
And ribald music
Circle around
A spangled lady.

(from 'Circus')
LOUIS MACNEICE

The Night-dawn Before the Last

The morning will drag itself up the walls
(long walls with no ending)
in the usual way.
Boots will crunch to a halt
outside the door.
No. They will recede again into the distance.
Three times today the air will be disturbed
by the smell of food.
The afternoon will crawl through
as afternoons do,
leaving the night to come.
The night
will pass as nights have passed before.
But then the customary circle
will be broken for me.
By a strand
of rope.

KEITH FISHER

Say this City

Say this city has ten million souls,
Some are living in mansions, some are living in holes:
Yet there's no place for us, my dear, yet there's no place for us.

Once we had a country and we thought it fair,
Look in the atlas and you'll find it there:
We cannot go there now, my dear, we cannot go there now.

In the village churchyard there grows an old yew,
Every spring it blossoms anew:
Old passports can't do that, my dear, old passports can't do that.

The consul banged the table and said:
'If you've got no passport you're officially dead':
But we are still alive, my dear, but we are still alive.

Went to a committee; they offered me a chair;
Asked me politely to return next year:
But where shall we go today, my dear, but where shall we go
    today?

Came to a public meeting; the speaker got up and said:
'If we let them in they will steal our daily bread';
He was talking of you and me, my dear, he was talking of you
    and me.

Thought I heard the thunder rumbling in the sky;
It was Hitler over Europe, saying: 'They must die';
O we were in his mind, my dear, O we were in his mind.

Saw a poodle in a jacket fastened with a pin,
Saw a door opened and a cat let in:
But they weren't German Jews, my dear, but they weren't
    German Jews.

Went down the harbour and stood upon the quay,
Saw the fish swimming as if they were free:
Only ten feet away, my dear, only ten feet away.

Walked through a wood, saw the birds in the trees;
They had no politicians and sang at their ease:
They weren't the human race, my dear, they weren't the human
    race.

Dreamed I saw a building with a thousand floors,
A thousand windows and a thousand doors;
Not one of them was ours, my dear, not one of them was ours.

Stood on a great plain in the falling snow;
Ten thousand soldiers marched to and fro:
Looking for you and me, my dear, looking for you and me.

W. H. AUDEN

Foodless Children

Foodless Children,
With stomachs puffed out,
Why have you no food to eat?
Why do you beg?

Foodless Children,
Suffering from starvation,
Why is your skin like paper?
Why do your bones poke out?

Foodless Children,
Eaten up by disease,
Why not see a doctor?
Why not?

Foodless Children,
You are so thin,
Your eyes are so appealing,
And you will soon be dead.

MALDWYN DAVIES

Psalm of Those Who Go Forth Before Daylight

The policeman buys shoes slow and careful; the teamster buys gloves slow and careful; they take care of their feet and hands; they live on their feet and hands.

The milkman never argues; he works alone and no one speaks to him; the city is asleep when he is on the job; he puts a bottle on six hundred porches and calls it a day's work; he climbs two hundred wooden stairways; two horses are company for him; he never argues.

The rolling-mill men and the sheet-steel men are brothers of cinders; they empty cinders out of their shoes after the day's work; they ask their wives to fix burnt holes in the knees of their trousers; their necks and ears are covered with a smut; they scour their necks and ears; they are brothers of cinders.

CARL SANDBURG

People

I like people quite well
at a little distance.
I like to see them passing and passing
and going their own way,
especially if I see their aloneness alive in them.
Yet I don't want them to come near.
If they will only leave me alone
I can still have the illusion that there is room enough in the world.

D. H. LAWRENCE

The Hunchback in the Park

The hunchback in the park
A solitary mister
Propped between trees and water
From the opening of the garden lock
That lets the trees and water enter
Until the Sunday sombre bell at dark

Eating bread from a newspaper
Drinking water from the chained cup
That the children filled with gravel
In the fountain basin where I sailed my ship
Slept at night in a dog kennel
But nobody chained him up.

Like the park birds he came early
Like the water he sat down
And Mister they called Hey mister
The truant boys from the town
Running when he had heard them clearly
On out of sound

Past lake and rockery
Laughing when he shook his paper
Hunchbacked in mockery
Through the loud zoo of the willow groves
Dodging the park keeper
With his stick that picked up leaves.

And the old dog sleeper
Alone between nurses and swans
While the boys among willows
Made the tigers jump out of their eyes
To roar on the rockery stones
And the groves were blue with sailors

Made all day until bell time
A woman figure without fault
Straight as a young elm
Straight and tall from his crooked bones
That she might stand in the night
After the locks and chains

All night in the unmade park
After the railings and shrubberies
The birds the grass the trees the lake
And the wild boys innocent as strawberries
Had followed the hunchback
To his kennel in the dark.

DYLAN THOMAS

I Asked an Old Man

I asked an old man for a light.
He shivered,
Looking for an old lighter
That bent his nimble thumb

Every time he pushed the wheel round.
    Suddenly the sun dropped and disappeared
    Into the misty lake of clouds.
    I saw an old lady across the road.
    She fell on her knees
    For a penny.

J. BUSSEY

The Dunce

He says no with his head
but he says yes with his heart
he says yes to what he loves
he says no to the teacher
he stands
he is questioned
and all the problems are posed
sudden laughter seizes him
and he erases all
the words and figures
names and dates
sentences and snares
and despite the teacher's threats
to the jeers of infant prodigies
with chalk of every colour
on the blackboard of misfortune
he draws the face of happiness.

JACQUES PRÉVERT
translated by Lawrence Ferlinghetti

Will Consider Situation

These here are words of radical advice for a young man looking
    for a job;
Young man, be a snob.
Yes, if you are in search of arguments against starting at the
    bottom,
Why I've gottom.
Let the personnel managers differ;
It's obvious that you will get on faster at the top than at the
    bottom because there are more people at the bottom than at
    the top so naturally the competition at the bottom is stiffer.
If you need any further proof that my theory works,
Well, nobody can deny that presidents get paid more than vice-
    presidents and vice-presidents get paid more than clerks.
Stop looking at me quizzically;
I want to add that you will never achieve fortune in a job that
    makes you uncomfortable physically.
When anybody tells you that hard jobs are better for you than
    soft jobs be sure to repeat this text to them,
Postmen tramp around all day through rain and snow just to
    deliver people's in cosy air-conditioned offices checks to
    them.
You don't need to interpret tea leaves stuck in a cup
To understand that people who work sitting down get paid more
    than people who work standing up.
Another thing about having a comfortable job is you not only
    accumulate more treasure;
You get more leisure.
So that when you find that you have worked so comfortably that
    your waistline is a menace,
You correct it with golf or tennis.
Whereas if in an uncomfortable job like piano-moving or
    stevedoring you indulge,
You have no time to exercise, you just continue to bulge.

To sum it up, young man, there is every reason to refuse a job
    that will make heavy demands on you corporally or manually,
And the only intelligent way to start your career is to accept a
    sitting position paying at least twenty-five thousand dollars
    annually.

OGDEN NASH

The One That Got Away

Don't talk to me about the one
That got away. You should
'Ave seen wot 'appened.
There I was, sitting there wiv me
Rod in one 'and, and a sammidge
In the uver, minding me own
Business and then it 'appened.
Me old reel started flying round and
Me old rod bent over and then
Ping!
The bloody lot 'ad gone.
All me line 'ad gone orf me
Reel and me rod was still shaking
From the vibrashun w'en me line went
And me rod flicked back.
I was flabbergasted! I just sat
There wiv 'alf a sammidge in me
'And, and me mouf wide open.

LESLIE PICKETT

Soldier Freddy

Soldier Freddy
    was never ready,
But! Soldier Neddy,
    unlike Freddy
Was *always* ready
    and steady,

That's why,
    When Soldier Neddy
Is-outside-Buckingham-Palace-on-guard-in-the
                pouring-wind-and-rain-
            being-steady-and-ready,
      Freddie—
        is home in beddy.

                SPIKE MILLIGAN

No Sale

All this year we've hardly turned a wheel. Trading's as slow as
    a funeral.
Talk about funerals: chap came in here this morning;
Jew: you could tell by his nose flying out of his face like a
    spinnaker;
Looks over the stock.
'Tell you what I want,' he said; 'car with a long chassis;
Don't see anything here very suitable.'
"Long chassis?" I said. I showed him the Studebaker.
"You don't want anything longer than that," I said,
"Surely," I said. 'Well,' he said, 'it don't look long enough to me.'
"Don't want to seem curious," I said; "but what do you want
    it for?"

'Funeral director,' he said, 'and I want a long chassis
To build a new hearse on; but that don't look long enough.'
"Now look here," I said; "you ever see a hearse
With a longer chassis than that Studebaker?
Cut her off at the front seat and look at all the space you've got."
'Can't see it,' he said; 'but listen, I'll tell you what:
You: you're as long in the legs as anyone I ever dealt with:
Just lie along her yourself, and let's see how she looks.'
"Time enough for that," I said; "time enough for that;
I'm no Grecian statue, I know, but I don't have to take on
Posing for stiffs, yet." I just couldn't do it. I'm not superstitious.
Or am I? The Jews, now: they bury them head to the west,
Don't they? Or head to the east, is it?
Do they put them head-first in the hearses?
I forget. I suppose it don't matter.
The hearse is the same size, in any case.
Perhaps he'll come back in the morning.
There's no longer car in the city at present that I've seen.

RONALD MCCUAIG

Mr Flood's Party

Old Eben Flood, climbing alone one night
Over the hill between the town below
And the forsaken upland hermitage
That held as much as he should ever know
On earth again of home, paused warily.
The road was his with not a native near;
And Eben, having leisure, said aloud,
For no man else in Tilbury Town to hear:

'Well, Mr Flood, we have the harvest moon
Again, and we may not have many more;
The bird is on the wing, the poet says,
And you and I have said it here before.

Drink to the bird.' He raised up to the light
The jug that he had gone so far to fill,
And answered huskily: 'Well, Mr Flood,
Since you propose it, I believe I will.'

Alone, as if enduring to the end
A valiant armor of scarred hopes outworn,
He stood there in the middle of the road
Like Roland's ghost winding a silent horn.
Below him, in the town among the trees,
Where friends of other days had honoured him,
A phantom salutation of the dead
Rang thinly till old Eben's eyes were dim.

Then, as a mother lays her sleeping child
Down tenderly, fearing it may awake,
He set the jug down slowly at his feet
With trembling care, knowing that most things break;
And only when assured that on firm earth
It stood, as the uncertain lives of men
Assuredly did not, he paced away,
And with his hand extended paused again:

'Well, Mr Flood, we have not met like this
In a long time; and many a change has come
To both of us, I fear since last it was
We had a drop together. Welcome home!'
Convivially returning with himself,
Again he raised the jug up to the light;
And with an acquiescent quaver said:
'Well, Mr Flood, if you insist, I might.

'Only a very little, Mr Flood—
For auld lang syne. No more, sir; that will do.'
So, for the time, apparently it did,
And Eben evidently thought so too;

For soon amid the silver loneliness
Of night he lifted up his voice and sang,
Secure, with only two moons listening,
Until the whole harmonious landscape rang—

'For auld lang syne.' The weary throat gave out,
The last word wavered, and the song was done.
He raised again the jug regretfully
And shook his head, and was again alone.
There was not much that was ahead of him,
And there was nothing in the town below—
Where strangers would have shut the many doors
That many friends had opened long ago.

EDWIN ARLINGTON ROBINSON

Past P.M.

My windows are leaded.
Twenty yards in front
Through the night deep
Roar satanic lonely lorries,
Drivers anonymous, hunched
With instruments glowing,
Dressed in assorted old clothes,
A creased, greasy, leather jacket
Finger nails broken and neglected,
They are alone.

Three minutes before, I
Hear the diesel whisper its
Protest, and sense the twin beams
Swing round corners,
And group ahead.

Thrust aside the sheets,
Change,
And rush down
To the road,
In time
For the blasting truck
Briefly to illuminate me,
And shudder to a halt.

The cab smells hot and oily
As the dawn breaks gently. . . .

ANGELA PARSONS

On the Move

'*Man, you gotta Go.*'

The blue jay scuffling in the bushes follows
Some hidden purpose, and the gust of birds
That spurts across the field, the wheeling swallows,
Have nested in the trees and undergrowth.
Seeking their instinct, or their poise, or both,
One moves with an uncertain violence
Under the dust thrown by a baffled sense
Or the dull thunder of approximate words.

On motorcycles, up the road, they come:
Small, black, as flies hanging in heat, the Boys,
Until the distance throws them forth, their hum
Bulges to thunder held by calf and thigh.
In goggles, donned impersonality,
In gleaming jackets trophied with the dust,
They strap in doubt—by hiding it, robust—
And almost hear a meaning in their noise.

Exact conclusion of their hardiness
Has no shape yet, but from known whereabouts
They ride, direction where the tires press.
They scare a flight of birds across the field:
Much that is natural, to the will must yield.
Men manufacture both machine and soul,
And use what they imperfectly control
To dare a future from the taken routes.

It is a part solution, after all.
One is not necessarily discord
On earth; or damned because, half animal
One lacks direct instinct, because one wakes
Afloat on movement that divides and breaks.
One joins the movement in a valueless world,
Choosing it, till, both hurler and the hurled,
One moves as well, always toward, toward.

A minute holds them, who have come to go:
The self-defined, astride the created will
They burst away; the towns they travel through
Are home for neither bird nor holiness,
For birds and saints complete their purposes.
At worst, one is in motion; and at best,
Reaching no absolute, in which to rest,
One is always nearer by not keeping still.

THOM GUNN

A Town Night

There is a last rush of people
Going home to their security.
Then the night gets darker,
The lights start to go on,

The sodium lamps move from
Red to dull orange.
The stragglers fade away.
At last there is solitude.

The hard street lights glare out,
Broken only by the red glow
Of a lamp that has not gone on properly.
A train moves in the underground below
And the ground vibrates.
The light in an upstairs window goes on,
Only to go off a few seconds later.
The city struggles to sleep.

The night moves on
Past midnight,
Without even knowing
What the word means.

TREVOR CLARKE

Leather-jackets, Bikes and Birds

The streets are noisy
with the movement of passing motors.
The coffee bars get fuller.
The leather-jacket groups begin to gather,
stand, and listen, pretending they are
looking for trouble.
The juke box plays its continuous
tune, music appreciated by Most.
The aroma of Espresso
coffee fills the nostrils and
the night.
Motorbikes pull up.

Riders dismount and join
their friends in the gang.
They stand, smoking, swearing,
playing with the girls;
making a teenage row.
They pretend not to notice the drizzle
falling out of the dark,
because you've got to be hard to
be a leather-jacket.
A couple
in a corner, snogging,
hope the motor lights will not be
dipped too much,
so that the others will see them.
They must all have recognition;
there must always be enough
leather-jackets around them,
the same as theirs.
The street lamp on the side
of the street shows the rain
for what it is—wet and cold.
But it does not show their faces
for what they are.

ROBERT DAVIES

Night Patrol

We sail at dusk. The red moon,
Rising in a paper lantern, sets fire
To the water; the black headland disappears
Into its own shadow, clenched like a paw.

The docks grow flat, rubbered with mist.
Cranes, like useless arms, hang
Over the railway. The unloading of coal
Continues under harsh arc-lights.

Turning south, the moon like a rouged face
Between masts, the knotted aerials swing
Taut against the horizon, the bag
Of sea crumpled in the spray-flecked blackness.

Towards midnight the cold stars, high
Over Europe, freeze on the sky,
Stigmata above the flickering lights
Of Holland. Flashes of gunfire

Lick out over meditative coastlines, betraying
The stillness. Taking up my position, night falls
Exhausted about us. The wakes
Of gunboats sew the green dark with speed.

From Dunkirk red flames open fanwise
In fingers of light; like the rising moon
Setting fire to the sky, the remote
Image of death burns on the water.

The slow tick of hours. Clouds grow visible.
Altering course the moon congeals on a new
Bearing. Northwards again, and Europe recedes
With the first sharp splinters of dawn.

The orange sky lies over the harbour,
Derricks and pylons like scarecrows
Black in the early light. And minesweepers
Pass us, moving out slowly to the North Sea.

ALAN ROSS

Exposure

Our brains ache, in the merciless iced east winds that knive us . . .
Wearied we keep awake because the night is silent . . .
Low, drooping flares confuse our memory of the salient . . .
Worried by silence, sentries whisper, curious, nervous,
    But nothing happens.

Watching, we hear the mad gusts tugging on the wire,
Like twitching agonies of men among its brambles.
Northward, incessantly, the flickering gunnery rumbles,
Far off, like a dull rumour of some other war.
    What are we doing here?

The poignant misery of dawn begins to grow . . .
We only know war lasts, rain soaks, and clouds sag stormy.
Dawn massing in the east her melancholy army
Attacks once more in ranks on shivering ranks of gray,
    But nothing happens.

Sudden successive flights of bullets streak the silence.
Less deadly than the air that shudders black with snow,
With sidelong flowing flakes that flock, pause, and renew,
We watch them wandering up and down the wind's nonchalance,
    But nothing happens.

Pale flakes with fingering stealth come feeling for our faces—
We cringe in holes, back on forgotten dreams, and stare,
  snow-dazed,
Deep into grassier ditches. So we drowse, sun-dozed,
Littered with blossoms trickling where the blackbird fusses.
    Is it that we are dying?

Slowly our ghosts drag home: glimpsing the sunk fires, glozed
With crusted dark-red jewels; crickets jingle there;
For hours the innocent mice rejoice: the house is theirs;

75

Shutters and doors, all closed: on us the doors are closed,—
  We turn back to our dying.

Since we believe not otherwise can kind fires burn;
Nor even suns smile true on child, or field, or fruit.
For God's invincible spring our love is made afraid;
Therefore, not loath, we lie out here; therefore were born,
  For love of God seems dying.

Tonight, His frost will fasten on this mud and us,
Shrivelling many hands, puckering foreheads crisp.
The burying-party, picks and shovels in their shaking grasp,
Pause over half-known faces. All their eyes are ice,
  But nothing happens.

                                        WILFRED OWEN

Assault

Gas!
faces turned,
eyes scanned the sky,
hands feverishly ripped open cannisters,
and masks were soon covering faces.
A man choked
as the white cloud,
swirling round him like fog, caught him
unawares.
Then his body flopped over.
Shells floated across
as if suspended by hidden strings,
and then, tired,
they sank earthwards.

A command!
I fixed my bayonet,
scrambled over the open trench,
and struggled through
the thick pasty mud.

It was quiet
as we walked
except for the sucking,
groaning, squelching sound
which came from the wet earth
as it tried
to creep into our stockings.
The wind cut me.

Over the wall!
Then a whistle.
'Good luck, mates.'
Mind that hole. Through the wire.
Over the top.
And kill.
'God. This is fun!'

ERNO MULLER

Hiroshima

Noon, and hazy heat;
A single silver sliver and a dull drone;
The gloved finger poised, pressed:
A second's silence, and
Oblivion.   ANON.

Fallen Tree

Barbaric relic of an ancient storm
Defiantly withstanding decomposition
Waiting with an outflung gesture of grey-white arms.

CAROL LITTLEWOOD

Rain on Dry Ground

That is rain on dry ground. We heard it:
We saw the little tempest in the grass,
The panic of anticipation: heard
The uneasy leaves flutter, the air pass
In a wave, the fluster of the vegetation;

Heard the first spatter of drops, the outriders
Larruping on the road, hitting against
The gate of the drought, and shattering
On to the lances of the tottering meadow.
It is rain; it is rain on dry ground.

Rain riding suddenly out of the air,
Battering the bare walls of the sun.
It is falling on to the tongue of the blackbird,
Into the heart of the thrush; the dazed valley
Sings it down. Rain, rain on dry ground!

This is the urgent decision of the day,
The urgent drubbing of earth, the urgent raid
On the dust; downpour over the flaring poppy,
Deluge on the face of noon, the flagellant
Rain drenching across the air.—The day

Flows in the ditch; bubble and twisting twig
And the sodden morning swirl along together

Under the crying hedge. And where the sun
Ran on the scythes, the rain runs down
The obliterated field, the blunted crop.

The rain stops.
The air is sprung with green.
The intercepted drops
Fall at their leisure; and between
The threading runnels on the slopes
The snail drags his caution into the sun.

CHRISTOPHER FRY

Coming

On longer evenings,
Light, chill and yellow,
Bathes the serene
Foreheads of houses.
A thrush sings,
Laurel-surrounded
In the deep bare garden,
Its fresh-peeled voice
Astonishing the brickwork.
It will be spring soon,
It will be spring soon—
And I, whose childhood
Is a forgotten boredom,
Feel like a child
Who comes on a scene
Of adult reconciling,
And can understand nothing
But the unusual laughter,
And starts to be happy.

PHILIP LARKIN

F

79

Spring Day

Something's going to happen today.
You can feel it.
The biting wind blows shiftingly
and there's a tingling in the air.
The usually drowsy factory smoke
now flows, uneasy through the twisting atmosphere.

BARRY RAPLEY

Quiet

The night was so quiet
That the hum of the candle burning
Came to my ear,
A sound of breath drawn through a reed
Far off.

The night was so quiet
That the air in the room
Poised, waiting to crack
Like a straining
Stick.

The night was so quiet
That the blood and flesh,
My visible self sunk in the chair,
Was a power-house giant, pulsing
Through the night.

RICHARD CHURCH

Just Two People

Through the darkened
Streets they walked,
Brightened with their
Love for each other.
On into the
Night for
All to see.
But to themselves
They are alone.

TONY JARDINE

Waiting

My love will come
will fling open her arms and fold me in them,
will understand my fears, observe my changes.
In from the pouring dark, from the pitch night
without stopping to bang the taxi door
she'll run upstairs through the decaying porch
burning with love and love's happiness,
she'll run dripping upstairs, she won't knock,
will take my head in her hands,
and when she drops her overcoat on a chair,
it will slide to the floor in a blue heap.

YEVGENY YEVTUSHENKO
translated by Robin Milner-Gulland
and Peter Levi, S.J.

Shame

Alone on Monday night, walking away
    from a fight I never had.
I feel lonely walking down the
    murky lane.
I can't feel my feet prodding along
    the road because I have other
    things to think about.
Why, why was I so terrified
    of somebody who was no bigger
    than me?
Whose face I'll never forget, his eyes
    pounding into my face.
Whose voice was so sharp and
    clear, that it made me shiver.
I walk away ashamed.

MALCOLM CRAGG

Journey Through the Night

At the first hour from dawn
The traveller in the window seat
Rubbed his eyes, woke from a daze,
Brushed his rough hair back with great
Podgy fingers, gave a yawn,
Cleared the pane's white dewy haze,
Then stared so eagerly, it might
Have been his home place come in sight.

But at the second hour from dawn
The traveller in the window seat
Suddenly turned away from the world
As though he saw some thing too sweet
Or too bitter to be borne;

And when he met my glance, he curled
His body to the wall, and wept
I thought; but it may be he slept.

At the third hour from dawn
The ticket man rolled back the door:
The traveller blurted out that he
Wanted another ticket for
Some other place, somewhere further on;
He spoke shortly, confusedly;
But I saw he did not know,
Now, where in the world to go.

JOHN HOLLOWAY

Good Taste

Travelling, a man met a tiger, so . . .
He ran. The tiger ran after him
Thinking: How fast I run . . . But

The road thought: How long I am . . . Then,
They came to a cliff, yes, the man
Grabbed at an ash root and swung down

Over its edge. Above his knuckles, the tiger.
At the foot of the cliff, its mate. Two mice,
One black, one white, began to gnaw the root.

And by the traveller's head grew one
Juicy strawberry, so . . . hugging the root
The man reached out and plucked the fruit.

How sweet it tasted!

CHRISTOPHER LOGUE

THREE

Look, Stranger

Look, stranger, on this island now
The leaping light for your delight discovers,
Stand stable here
And silent be,
That through the channels of the ear
May wander like a river
The swaying sound of the sea.

Here at the small field's ending pause
When the chalk wall falls to the foam and its tall ledges
Oppose the pluck
And knock of the tide,
And the shingle scrambles after the sucking surf,
And the gull lodges
A moment on its sheer side.

Far off like floating seeds the ships
Diverge on urgent voluntary errands,
And the full view
Indeed may enter
And move in memory as now these clouds do,
That pass the harbour mirror
And all the summer through the water saunter.

W. H. AUDEN

Broom

The thick scent of broom fills the air
Blue sky hangs over dusty chalk
The white hill sand breathes heat
Blue butterflies hover over misty scabious
The soft wildness of their flowers
Sweetens their spiky foliage
Yellow ragwort, red robin
And multi-coloured shells of creeping snails
Their life is the sun and the chalk:
The dry powder whiteness of the air
Shimmering with broom-filled heat.
The broom sends forth its power,
The fragrance of those soft and yellow flowers,
The shape and texture of the dark green leaves,
Over the heat of the chalk,
The feel of the grass;
The call of the lapwing.
The snails form burrows,
The ragwort comes to seed
And blows away its silken heads
From golden fingers of its flowers
The dock stems redden, their tiny fruit
Green and red of the sound of the heat
Fall and scatter; but the broom stays.
Clouds of wasps, follies of moths
Belong to the broom, the blueness of heat,
The life of the sun on the chalk baked hills
And they live for the broom, as the broom
                            for the sun
On the tough dried grass and the haze
                    of white chalk
And the scent of the broom breathes on
                    the chalk.

HELEN CLAIRE MILEFANTI

85

Florence: Design for a City

Take one bowl, one valley
Assisted by hills to peace
And let the hills hold back the wind a little
Only turning the trees
Only dividing the shadows
With a simple movement of sun
Across the valley's face.

And then set cypresses up,
So dark they seem to contain their repeated shadows
In a straight and upward leap,
So dark that the sun seems to avoid them to show
How austere they are, stiff, admonishing gestures
Towards the city, yet also protective
To the deep houses that the sun makes more deep.

Here I say the mind is open, is freed;
Anchored only to frailest thoughts, we are
Triumphantly subdued to the light's full glare.
It is simple then to be a stranger,
To have a mind that is wide
To permit the city to settle between our thoughts,
And between those hills, and flower and glow inside.

ELIZABETH JENNINGS

The White Stick

Red bricks, grey slate, cream road.
My eyes ached.
Same old walls, same old houses,
Old churches, old shops, old railings,
Everything was old,
No grass or trees.

86

I was sick, for want of the country;
I looked around me,
My eyes were drawn
To a solitary figure, walking, slowly.
I saw in the figure's hand a white stick—
Blindness.
I imagined the eternal blackness.
What had he done
To earn this mockery of man?
The figure turned into another street,
Tapping, feeling for the next shape,
Dependent on the white stick.
I wanted to help him.
What use was I? Just to show him the next corner.

PETER WINGATE

Ray Charles

In his dark dark world
The light comes through
His voice and harmony; his light.
He wails,
Man how he wails,
The groan,
And this is his light.
The beat
The food of light
The scream.
The nectar.
And he wails
The light gets lighter
He moves in his lonely world
Faster, Faster.
The groan, the wail, the scream.

87

They scream
He screams
The light dims
He is alone
In his dark dark world
Until his voice
Brings light to his soul.

ROBERT LEWIS

Elvis Presley

Two minutes long it pitches through some bar:
Unreeling from a corner box, the sign
Of this one, in his gangling finery
And crawling sideburns, wielding a guitar.

The limitations where he found success
Are ground on which he, panting, stretches out
In turn, promiscuously, by every note,
Our idiosyncrasy and our likeness.

We keep ourselves in touch with a mere dime:
Distorting hackneyed words in hackneyed songs
He turns revolt into a style, prolongs
The impulse to a habit of the time.

Whether he poses or is real, no cat
Bothers to say: the pose held is a stance,
Which, generation of the very chance
It wars on, may be posture for combat.

THOM GUNN

Boomlay

Fat black bucks in a wine-barrel room,
Barrel-house kings, with feet unstable,
Sagged and reeled and pounded on the table,
Pounded on the table,
Beat an empty barrel with the handle of a broom,
Hard as they were able,
Boom, boom, boom,
With a silk umbrella and the handle of a broom,
Boomlay, boomlay, boomlay, BOOM.
Then I had religion, then I had a vision,
I could not turn from their revel in derision.
Then I saw the Congo, creeping through the black,
Cutting through the forest with a golden track.
Then along that riverbank
A thousand miles
Tattooed cannibals danced in files;
Then I heard the boom of the blood-lust song
And a thigh-bone beating on a tin-pan gong.
And 'Blood' screamed the whistles and the fifes of the warriors,
'Blood' screamed the skull-faced lean witch doctors,
'Whirl ye the deadly voo-doo rattle,
Harry the uplands,
Steal all the cattle,
Rattle-rattle, rattle-rattle,
Bing.
Boomlay, boomlay, boomlay, Boom,'
A roaring, epic, rag-time tune
From the mouth of the Congo
To the mountains of the Moon.

(From 'The Congo')
VACHEL LINDSAY

Nuit Blanche: North End

Red and green neon lights, the jazz hysteria,
for all-night movie and all-night cafeteria;
you feed all night in one, and sleep in the other,
and dream that a strip-tease queen was your sweetheart's mother.

A nickel for a coffee—half a dime for a seat;
the blondes and the guns are streamlined and complete;
streamlined, dreamlined, with wide open cactus spaces
between the four-foot teeth in the ten-foot faces.

Hot trumpets and hot trombones for a soft-sole shuffle!
Sailors, bring in your tattoos, park your duffel!
There's a green-tailed blue-eyed mermaid stinging my shoulder,
and I've got to pass out before I'm a minute older.

Sawdust, spittoon, no smoking, please excuse—
afloat or ashore we mind our p's and q's.
Longhorn stand back, shorthorn stand close, is all
the circular eye makes out on the circular wall.

And still the red neon lights go round and around,
the red mouth opens and drinks with never a sound,—
red on the Square, red on the jingling Palace,
where all night long you rumbaed and drank with Alice—

red on the tattoo artist's sign, that shakes
anchors and flags together, ships and snakes,
roses, and a pink Venus, on a shell,
la, la, all dancing feet in a neon hell—

while round and around the red beads wink, and faster
empty and open, pour and fill, disaster:
the red mouth opens and drinks, opens and winks,
drinks down the hotel wall, the drugstore, drinks

the Square, the statue, the bright red roofs of cabs,
and the cleaning-women, who arise with pails and swabs:
then stains the dawn, who, over the subway station,
steals in, with Sandals gray, but no elation.

CONRAD AIKEN

Naked

The one black figure
Broke the long, smooth line—
The line of sand.
The dust rose round his feet,
Small, yellow puffs, stirred by the dragging feet
Pulled listlessly on, across the rolling dunes.

The sun burned, seared
—blackened his naked skin
—blackened his naked mind
a long hot trail of emptiness
slow dragging footsteps, across the rolling dunes of yellow sand
Burning yellow streaks across a lonely mind.

JOHN HUMPHREYS

Colour Dream

The crimson lakes
    babbled in
the cold
      sun while
the blue moss
    saturated by
the   light
     rain
squelched under
       the strain
   of
tiny green
    roots
The orange trees
    whistled in
the breeze
      and their sooty
      leaves fell in a
heap
    to the
    ground
A yellow zebra
    bounded into
view
    followed by
    a purple lion
Through the
    red bracken
they hurled
      themselves
      to awake
on the verge
    of the crimson
lake.

PATRICIA LLOYD

92

Chanson Innocente

In Just—
spring   when the world is mud-
luscious the little
lame balloonman

whistles   far   and wee
and eddieandbill come
running from marbles and
piracies and it's
spring

when the world is puddle-wonderful

the queer
old balloonman whistles
far   and   wee
and bettyandisbel come dancing

from hop-scotch and jump-rope and

it's
spring
and
    the
        goat-footed

balloonMan   whistles
far
and
wee

E. E. CUMMINGS

To Paint the Portrait of a Bird

First paint a cage
with an open door
then paint
something pretty
something simple
something beautiful
something useful . . .
for the bird
then place the canvas against a tree
in a garden
in a wood
or in a forest
hide behind the tree
without speaking
without moving . . .
Sometimes the bird comes quickly
but he can just as well spend long years
before deciding
Don't get discouraged
wait
wait years if necessary
the swiftness or slowness of the coming
of the bird having no rapport
with the success of the picture
When the bird comes
if he comes
observe the most profound silence
wait till the bird enters the cage
and when he has entered
gently close the door with a brush
then
paint out all the bars one by one
taking care not to touch any of the feathers of the bird
Then paint the portrait of the tree

choosing the most beautiful of its branches
for the bird
paint also the green foliage and the wind's freshness
the dust of the sun
and the noise of insects in the summer heat
and then wait for the bird to decide to sing
If the bird doesn't sing
it's a bad sign
a sign that the painting is bad
but if he sings it's a good sign
a sign that you can sign
so then so very gently you pull out
one of the feathers of the bird
and you write your name in a corner of the picture.

JACQUES PRÉVERT
translated by Lawrence Ferlinghetti

Jealousy

I put out my hand and plucked a rose,
A red satin rose with a velvet scent,
And chaliced its loveliness in reverent palms,
Knowing that it was perfect.

Then, because I could not make the rose,
And because I could not paint the rose,
Nor carve it, nor mould it,
Nor even draw its beauty in my words,
I slowly closed my fingers over it
And crushed it.

RUTH ELLISON

Thoughts of Possession

I knew I could go, yet no,
I must wait and wait again.
Would she come, could I stay?
I couldn't think.
Now I saw her, a shadow dancing,
bouncing, beating, against the wall
lit with white light, as burning magnesium.
I ran to hold her, touch her hair
waving like seaweed under water.
I heard her footsteps, light as the beats
from a dove's wing.
I stretched my hand, my arm, my body
but I could not reach her, she was
so far, a gulf as the universe between
us.
Then a beat in my heart thrust me
forward, some clue, a hint, was I there?
Again I tried, stretched and writhed, but
no I could not reach her.
I fell back ashamed and broken.
I had failed, and, as a fool I cried.

WILLIAM HADDOCK

Dear, Though the Night is Gone

Dear, though the night is gone,
Its dream still haunts today,
That brought us to a room
Cavernous, lofty as
A railway terminus.
And crowded in that gloom
Were beds, and we in one
In a far corner lay.

Our whisper woke no clocks,
We kissed and I was glad
At everything you did,
Indifferent to those
Who sat with hostile eyes
In pairs on every bed,
Arms round each other's neck,
Inert and vaguely sad.

O but what worm of guilt
Or what malignant doubt
Am I the victim of,
That you then, unabashed,
Did what I never wished,
Confessed another love;
And I, submissive, felt
Unwanted and went out?

W. H. AUDEN

One Afternoon

It was a most beautiful
afternoon.
The rich smell of the long green grass
was overpowering.
And we lay in the long green
grass.
And felt the soft caress of the blades.
It was so quiet
we could almost hear the billowing of the
clouds.
As we lay in the long green grass
hand in hand.
Then we kissed
quickly.

And for a moment we were able to leave
this world of hate and
sorrow.
Then we kissed again
and this time you kissed hard and greedily
in the beauty and
quiet
of the afternoon and the long green grass.
And a feeling of nausea
came over me—
because you had spoilt it all by being
greedy.

MARTIN PEPLER

Woman to Man

The eyeless labourer in the night,
the selfless, shapeless seed I hold,
builds for its resurrection day—
silent and swift and deep from sight
foresees the unimagined light.

This is no child with a child's face;
this has no name to name it by:
yet you and I have known it well.
This our hunter and our chase,
the third who lay in our embrace.

This is the strength that your arm knows,
the arc of flesh that is my breast,
the precise crystals of our eyes.
This is the blood's wild tree that grows
the intricate and folded rose.

This is the maker and the made;
this is the question and reply;
the blind head butting at the dark,
the blaze of light along the blade.
Oh hold me, for I am afraid.

JUDITH WRIGHT

Deceptions

'Of course I was drugged, and so heavily I did not regain my
consciousness till the next morning. I was horrified to discover
that I had been ruined, and for some days I was inconsolable and
cried like a child to be killed or sent back to my aunt.'—Mayhew,
'London Labour and the London Poor.'

Even so distant, I can taste the grief,
Bitter and sharp with stalks, he made you gulp.
The sun's occasional print, the brisk brief
Worry of wheels along the street outside
Where bridal London bows the other way,
And light, unanswerable and tall and wide,
Forbids the scar to heal, and drives
Shame out of hiding. All the unhurried day
Your mind lay open like a drawer of knives.

Slums, years, have buried you. I would not dare
Console you if I could. What can be said,
Except that suffering is exact, but where
Desire takes charge, readings will grow erratic?
For you would hardly care
That you were less deceived, out on that bed,
Than he was, stumbling up the breathless stair
To burst into fulfilment's desolate attic.

PHILIP LARKIN

Under the Olives

We never would have loved had love not struck
Swifter than reason, and despite reason:
Under the olives, our hands interlocked,
We both fell silent:
Each listened for the other's answering
Sigh of unreasonableness—
Innocent, gentle, bold, enduring, proud.

ROBERT GRAVES

Night Ride

Along the black
leather strap
of the night
deserted road

swiftly rolls
the freighted bus.
Huddled together
two lovers doze

their hands linkt
across their laps
their bodies loosely
interlockt

their heads resting
two heavy fruits
on the plaited
basket of their limbs.

Slowly the bus
slides into the light.

Here are hills
detach'd from dark

the road, uncoils
a white ribbon
the lovers with
the hills unfold

wake cold
to face the fate
of those who love
despite the world.

HERBERT READ

Midnight on the Great Western

In the third-class seat sat the journeying boy,
      And the roof-lamp's oily flame
Played down on his listless form and face,
Bewrapt past knowing to what he was going,
            Or whence he came.

In the band of his hat the journeying boy
      Had a ticket stuck; and a string
Around his neck bore the key of his box,
That twinkled gleams of the lamp's sad beams
            Like a living thing.

What past can be yours, O journeying boy
      Towards a world unknown,
Who calmly, as if incurious quite
On all at stake, can undertake
            This plunge alone?

Knows your soul a sphere, O journeying boy,
    Our rude realms far above,
Whence with spacious vision you mark and mete
This region of sin that you find you in,
    But are not of?

THOMAS HARDY

Trio

The way was dark,
The night was lonely,
As two travellers struggled through their journey.
Presently they were joined by a third person
Who seemed to appear from nowhere.
The three made friends,
And soon got talking;
Talking about religion
And the Son of God.
At times the first two travellers were almost arguing,
While the third remained quiet—
(A young man with fair hair and beard).
But the journey was too long to talk
All the time.
Then the lonely night and the dark way were silent.
As the weary travellers neared the town
With its noise and lights
The late arrival disappeared
Just as quickly as he had come,
Leaving the two men
Amazed.
They searched the place about them,
But the person had disappeared
As imperceptibly as the silence.
That night at the inn

As the two travellers,
Tired and weary-limbed,
Were in their warm beds,
They thought of the silence and of the silent and
Strange young man who had joined them on the road.

VICTOR HARRIS

Journey of the Magi

'A cold coming we had of it,
Just the worst time of the year
For a journey, and such a long journey:
The ways deep and the weather sharp,
The very dead of winter.'
And the camels galled, sore-footed, refractory,
Lying down in the melting snow.
There were times we regretted
The summer palaces on slopes, the terraces,
And the silken girls bringing sherbet.
Then the camel men cursing and grumbling
And running away, and wanting their liquor and women,
And the night-fires going out, and the lack of shelters,
And the cities hostile and the towns unfriendly
And the villages dirty and charging high prices:
A hard time we had of it.
At the end we preferred to travel all night,
Sleeping in snatches,
With the voices singing in our ears, saying
That this was all folly.

Then at dawn we came down to a temperate valley,
Wet, below the snow line, smelling of vegetation;
With a running stream and a water mill beating the darkness,
And three trees on the low sky,
And an old white horse galloped away in the meadow.

Then we came to a tavern with vine leaves over the lintel,
Six hands at an open door dicing for pieces of silver,
And feet kicking the empty wine-skins.
But there was no information, and so we continued
And arrived at evening, not a moment too soon
Finding the place; it was (you may say) satisfactory.

All this was a long time ago, I remember,
And I would do it again, but set down
This set down
This: were we led all that way for
Birth or Death? There was a Birth, certainly,
We had evidence and no doubt. I had seen birth and death,
But had thought they were different; this Birth was
Hard and bitter agony for us, like Death, our death.
We returned to our places, these kingdoms,
But no longer at ease here, in the old dispensation,
With an alien people clutching their gods.
I should be glad of another death.

T. S. ELIOT

The Crown of Roses

When Jesus Christ was yet a child
He had a garden small and wild,
Wherein he cherished roses fair
And wove them into garlands there.

Now once as summer time drew nigh
There came a troop of children by,
And seeing roses on a tree,
With shouts they plucked them merrily.

'Do you bind roses in your hair?'
They cried in scorn to Jesus there.

The boy said humbly, 'Take I pray
All but the naked thorns away.'

Then of the thorns they made a crown,
And with rough fingers pressed it down,
Till on his forehead fair and young
Red drops of blood like roses sprung.

RUSSIAN CAROL

In the Wilderness

He, of his gentleness,
Thirsting and hungering
Walked in the wilderness;
Soft words of grace he spoke
Unto lost desert-folk
That listened wondering.
He heard the bittern call
From ruined palace-wall,
Answered him brotherly;
He held communion
With the she-pelican
Of lonely piety.
Basilisk, cockatrice,
Flocked to his homilies,
With mail of dread device,
With monstrous barbèd stings,
With eager dragon-eyes;
Great bats on leather wings
And poor blind broken things
Mean in their miseries.
Then ever with him went,
Of all his wanderings
Comrade with ragged coat,
Gaunt ribs,—poor innocent—

Bleeding foot, burning throat,
The guileless old scapegoat:
For forty nights and days
Followed in Jesus' ways,
Sure guard behind him kept,
Tears like a lover wept.

ROBERT GRAVES

Crucifixion

Strapped to a post,
clothes ripped off his back
he smiled
for they could not hurt him—
he was Christ.

But they whipped him and it hurt

Then came the cross
all shiny and clean
and he said to himself,
'This can't be real. For
my angels will come and take me away.'

But the angels in heaven
were asleep at the time

And he dropped his cross
three times in a mile

Till another Jew had to help him
up the last slope

And he stood there alone
a man without hope.

They nailed him that day
on to the cross, two men-thieves
beside him, the sheep of his
flock.

He was right about one thing, though,
for the angels that day
came down
and took him away.

ERNO MULLER

Death

Nor dread nor hope attend
A dying animal;
A man awaits his end
Dreading and hoping all;
Many times he died,
Many times rose again.
A great man in his pride
Confronting murderous men
Casts derision upon
Supersession of breath;
He knows death to the bone—
Man has created death.

W. B. YEATS

My Brother

I am in bed,
Nobody to talk to.
The bed next to me is naked—
Nobody is in it
Now he's dead,

Only five he was
Just a baby.
Whilst I write in my note book,
The wind howls
Now he's dead.
When he was a child I thought nothing of him,
But now he's dead I weep for him.
The pillow soaking wet with my tears—
I turned it over.
Sad that I am, I will forget him.
Why couldn't I die instead of him?
I turned on the radio to harden my heart,
But his favourite tune is on.
I will never forget him—
He's dead now.

PHILIP CAMPBELL

Message for My Father

I'm never certain what the message is
except that it is quiet and in words.
I watch you bending by the apple tree,
the white cloud massive as a watching head,
the dark earth gentle. Maybe time compels.
Or maybe time is all we have to spare.

I used to climb, once, a particular tree
under a stack side, and its upper twigs
wore crazy straws clawed from that stack I'd slide
and slither down most days, adept at falls
on to the gold ground, breathless, jumping up
to climb again and slide down from the sky.
But the tree. I think that it was bare,
or nearly bare, the mossed bark knuckled through,
the twigs dry. Certainly there were no apples.

Yet it lived. Transfigurations talked
crowded as sparrows on its bitten leaves.
If it had leaves. I can't remember quite.
Yes, leaves there must have been, for there was shade
poppling my face in sunlight. I would pick
one leaf and keep it like a word from home.

And so it comes round to it, slowly round,
nearing the message—if the leaf will speak,
if words and memories can be retrieved.
You're standing now, and easing your stiff back,
watching the Worcester Pearmains change the sky.
Yet how am I to say . . . what can't be said
except by silence? I talk silence out
until it comes back filled with every phrase
of hesitation, every false start,
the passion, the enquiry, and the love.

ROBIN SKELTON

My Joy, My Jockey, My Gabriel

My joy, my jockey, my Gabriel
Who bares his horns above my sleep
Is sleeping now. And I shall keep him
In valley and on pinnacle
And marvellous in my tabernacle.

My peace is where his shoulder holds
My clouds among his skies of face;
His plenty is my peace, my peace:
And like a serpent by a boulder
His shade I rest in glory coiled.

Time will divide us, and the sea
Wrings its wild hands all day between;
The autumn brings a change of scene.
But always and forever he
At night will sleep and keep by me.

GEORGE BARKER

Lance-corporal Dixon

I saw a picture in the paper the other day
Of a soldier carrying a baby.
Lance-corporal Dixon was his name.
The baby?
His C.O's daughter.
My mother was touched by the picture,
Said it was charming
That a man so tough
Could be so gentle.
It looked odd to me:
A sten gun under one arm,
A baby under the other.

LINDA NEWTON

Guided Missiles Experimental Range

Soft sounds and odours brim up through the night
A wealth below the level of the eye;
Out of a black, an almost violent sky
Abundance flowers into points of light.

Till from the south-west, as their low scream mars
And halts this warm hypnosis of the dark,

Three black automata cut swift and stark,
Shaped clearly by the backward flow of stars.

Stronger than lives, by empty purpose blinded,
The only thought their circuits can endure is
The target-hunting rigour of their flight;

And by that loveless haste I am reminded
Of Aeschylus' description of the Furies:
'O barren daughters of the fruitful night.'

ROBERT CONQUEST

This Age

Old, old buildings, bleak, misty and gripping.
New, new lights of white, far into the distance.
When will uncertainty ever cease? Never.
Pulled back into the past, backward.
Never to grip the future. Slipping.
Held in history always, always, always.
We are the most uncertain age of all.

PETER WINGATE

Wages

The wages of work is cash.
The wages of cash is want more cash.
The wages of want more cash is vicious competition.
The wages of vicious competition is—the world we live in.

The work-cash-want circle is the viciousest circle
that ever turned men into fiends.

Earning a wage is a prison occupation
and a wage-earner is a sort of gaol-bird.

Earning a salary is a prison overseer's job,
a gaoler instead of a gaol-bird.

Living on your income is strolling grandly outside the prison
in terror lest you have to go in. And since the work-prison covers
almost every scrap of the living earth, you stroll up and down
on a narrow beat, about the same as a prisoner taking his exercise.

This is called universal freedom.

D. H. LAWRENCE

warty bliggens the toad

i met a toad
the other day by the name
of warty bliggens
he was sitting under
a toadstool
feeling contented
he explained that when the cosmos
was created
that toadstool was especially
planned for his personal
shelter from sun and rain
thought out and prepared
for him

do not tell me
said warty bliggens
that there is not a purpose
in the universe
the thought is blasphemy
a little more
conversation revealed
that warty bliggens
considers himself to be

the centre of the said
universe
the earth exists
to grow toadstools for him
to sit under
the sun to give him light
by day and the moon
and wheeling constellations
to make beautiful
the night for the sake of
warty bliggens

to what act of yours
do you impute
this interest on the part
of the creator
of the universe
i asked him
why is it that you
are so greatly favoured

ask rather
said warty bliggens
what the universe
has done to deserve me
if i were a
human being i would
not laugh
too complacently
at poor warty bliggens
for similar
absurdities
have only too often
lodged in the crinkles
of the human cerebrum
                    archy.

DON MARQUIS

113

Dream and Thing

This is the thing, this truly is the thing.
We dreamt it once; now it has come about.
That was the dream, but this, this is the thing.
The dream was bold, and thought it could foretell
What time would bring, but time, it seems, can bring
Only this thing which never has had a doubt
That everything is much like everything,
And the deep family likeness will come out.
We thought the dream would spread its folded wing;
But here's a thing that's neither sick nor well,
Stupid nor wise, and has no story to tell,
Though every tale is about and about.
That is the thing, that is the very thing.
Yet take another look and you may bring
From the dull mass each separate splendour out.
There is no trust but in the miracle.

EDWIN MUIR

Echo

Nothing is lost, sweet self,
Nothing is ever lost.
The unspoken word
Is not exhausted but can be heard.
Music that stains
The silence remains
O echo is everywhere, the unbeckonable bird!

LAURENCE DURRELL

Epitaph

I think they will remember this as the age of lamentations,
The age of broken minds and broken souls,
The age of hurt creatures sobbing out their sorrow to the rhythm
    of the blues—
The music of lost Africa's desolation become the music of the
    town.

The age of failure of splendid things,
The age of the deformity of splendid things,
The age of old young men and bitter children,
The age of treachery and of a great new faith.
The age of madness and machines,
Of broken bodies and fear twisted hearts,

The age of frenzied fumbling and possessive lusts—
And yet, deep down, an age unsatisfied by dirt and guns,
An age which though choked by the selfishness of the few who
    owned their bodies and their souls,
Still struggled blindly to the end,
And in their time reached out magnificently
Even for the very stars themselves.

H. D. CARBERRY

Acknowledgements

We wish to thank the following for permission to reproduce copyright poems.

Conrad Aiken: from *Collected Poems*. Reprinted by permission of Brandt & Brandt.

W. H. Auden: from *Collected Poems 1927–1957*. Reprinted by permission of Faber and Faber Ltd.

George Barker: from *Collected Poems 1930–1955*. Reprinted by permission of Faber and Faber Ltd.

Bertolt Brecht: 'The Plum-Tree', translated by Edwin Morgan from *Critical Quarterly*, Winter 1959. Reprinted by permission of the author and the editor of the journal.

Audrey A. Brown: 'The Goldfish' from *All Fools' Day*. Reprinted by permission of McGraw-Hill Ryerson Ltd.

J. Bussey: 'I asked on Old Man' from *And When You Are Young*. Reprinted by permission of the London Association for the Teaching of English.

H. D. Carberry: 'Epitaph' from *The Treasury of Jamaican Verse*. Reprinted by permission of The Poetry League of Jamaica.

Richard Church: 'Quiet' from *Collected Poems*. Reprinted by permission of William Heinemann Ltd.

Robert Conquest: 'Guided Missiles Experimental Range' from *Poems*. Reprinted by permission of Macmillan, London and Basingstoke.

E. E. Cummings: 'Chanson Innocente' from *Selected Poems*. Reprinted by permission of Faber and Faber Ltd.

Lawrence Durrell: 'Echo' from *Collected Poems*. Reprinted by permission of Faber and Faber Ltd.

T. S. Eliot: 'Journey of the Magi' from *Collected Poems 1909–1962*. Reprinted by permission of Faber and Faber Ltd.

R. Ellison: 'Jealousy' from *And When You Are Young*. Reprinted by permission of the London Association for the Teaching of English.

S. Freer: 'Saturdays' from *And When You Are Young*. Reprinted by permission of the London Association for the Teaching of English.

Robert Frost: 'The Fear' and 'After Apple-Picking' from *The Poetry of Robert Frost*, ed. E. C. Lathem. Reprinted by permission of Jonathan Cape Ltd. The poems are also reprinted from *The Complete Poems of Robert Frost*. © 1930, 1939 by Holt, Rinehart and Winston, Inc. Copyright © 1958 by Robert Frost. Reprinted by permission of Holt, Rinehart and Winston, Inc.

Christopher Fry: 'Rain on Dry Ground' from *The Boy with a Cart*. Reprinted by permission of Frederick Muller Ltd.

Robert Graves: 'Under the Olives' from *More Poems* and 'Welsh Incident' and 'In the Wilderness' from *Collected Poems 1965*. Reprinted by permission of A. P. Watt and Son on behalf of Mr. Robert Graves.

Thom Gunn: 'On the Move' and 'Elvis Presley' from *The Sense of Movement*. Reprinted by permission of Faber and Faber Ltd.

Thomas Hardy: 'Midnight on the Great Western' from *Collected Poems*. Reprinted by permission of the Trustees of the Hardy Estate and Macmillan, London and Basingstoke.

John Holloway: 'Journey through the Night' from *The Minute*. Reprinted by permission of The Marvell Press.

Ted Hughes: 'Hawk Roosting' from *Lupercal*. Reprinted by permission of Faber and Faber Ltd. 'The Casualty' from *The Hawk in the Rain*. Copyright © 1957 by Ted Hughes. Reprinted by permission of Faber and Faber Ltd. and Harper and Row, Inc.

Elizabeth Jennings: 'Florence: Design for a City' from *A Way of Looking* (Andre Deutsch). Reprinted by permission of David Higham Associates Ltd.

James Kirkup: 'The Eve of Christmas' from *A Spring Journey* (OUP) reprinted by permission of the author.

Philip Larkin: 'Coming' and 'Deceptions' from *The Less Deceived*. Reprinted by permission of The Marvell Press.

D. H. Lawrence: 'People' and 'Wages' from *The Complete Poems*. Reprinted by permission of Lawrence Pollinger Ltd. and the Estate of the late Mrs. Frieda Lawrence.

Vachel Lindsay: 'Boomlay' from *Collected Poems*. Reprinted by permission of Macmillan Publishing Co., Inc.

Christopher Logue: 'Good Taste' from *Songs*. Reprinted by permission of the Hutchinson Publishing Group Ltd.

S. Longwill: 'Snow' and 'Overnight' from the *Daily Mirror Children's Literary Competition* Reprinted by permission of the author and the *Daily Mirror*.

Amy Lowell: 'Night Clouds' from *What's O'Clock*. Reprinted by permission of Houghton Mifflin Company.

Robert Lowell: 'My Last Afternoon with Uncle Devereux Winslow' from *Life Studies*. Copyright © 1959 by Robert Lowell. Reprinted by permission of Faber and Faber Ltd. and Farrar, Straus and Giroux, Inc.

Ronald McCuaig: 'No Sale' from *The Penguin Book of Australian Verse*. Reprinted by permission of the author.

Louis MacNeice: 'Christmas Shopping' and 'Horses' from *The Collected Poems*. Reprinted by permission of Faber and Faber Ltd.

Don Marquis: 'Warty bliggens the toad' from *Archy and Mehitabel*. Copyright 1927 by Doubleday & Co. Inc. Reprinted by permission of the publishers.

Edgar Lee Masters: 'Butch Weldy' from *Spoon River Anthology*. Reprinted by permission of Weissberger & Frosch on behalf of Mrs. E. L. Masters.

Ray Mathew: 'Our Father' from *The Penguin Book of Australian Verse*. Reprinted by permission of the author.

H. C. Milefanti: 'Broom' from the *Daily Mirror Children's Literary Competition*. Reprinted by permission of the author and the *Daily Mirror*.

Spike Milligan: 'Soldier Freddy' from *A Dustbin of Milligan*. Reprinted by permission of Dennis Dobson, Publishers.

Ogden Nash: 'Will Consider Situation'. Reprinted by permission of J. M. Dent & Sons Ltd.

Wilfred Noyce: 'Breathless' from *South Col*. Reprinted by permission of William Heinemann Ltd.

Wilfred Owen: 'Exposure'. Reprinted by permission of Chatto & Windus Ltd.

Angela Parsons: 'Past P.M.' from the *Daily Mirror Children's Literary Competition*. Reprinted by permission of the author and the *Daily Mirror*.

William Plomer: 'In the Snake Park' from *Collected Poems*. Reprinted by permission of Jonathan Cape Ltd.

Jacques Prevert: 'The Dunce' and 'To Paint the Portrait of a Bird' from *Paroles*, trans. Lawrence Ferlinghetti. Copyright © 1948 by Librairie Gallimard. Reprinted by permission of City Lights Books. 'Exercise Book' from *For Love and Money*, trans. Paul Dehn. Reprinted by permission of The Bodley Head.

Herbert Read: 'Night Ride' from *Collected Poems*. Reprinted by permission of Faber and Faber Ltd.

Henry Reed: 'Judging Distances' from *A Map of Verona*. Reprinted by permission of Jonathan Cape Ltd.

Edwin Arlington Robinson: 'Mr. Flood's Party' from *Collected Poems*. Reprinted by permission of the Macmillan Publishing Co., Inc.

Alan Ross: 'Night Patrol'. Reprinted by permission of Hamish Hamilton Ltd.

Carl Sandburg: 'Psalm of Those Who Go Forth before Daylight' from *Cornhuskers*. Copyright 1918 by Holt, Rinehart & Winston, Inc.; renewed, 1946, by Carl Sandburg. 'Fog' from *Chicago Poems*. Copyright 1916 by Holt, Rinehart & Winston Inc; renewed 1947 by Carl Sandburg. Reprinted by permission of Harcourt Brace Jovanovich, Inc.

Robin Skelton: 'Message for my Father' from *Critical Quarterly*, Spring 1960. Reprinted by permission of the author and the editor of the journal.

Bernard Spencer: 'On the Road' from *Penguin New Writing* 1947. Reprinted by permission of Alan Ross Ltd.

Stephen Spender: 'The Pylons' from *Collected Poems*. Reprinted by permission of Faber and Faber Ltd.

Dylan Thomas: 'Fern Hill' and 'The Hunchback in the Park'. Reprinted by permission of J. M. Dent & Sons Ltd.

C. J. Turner: 'Holiday' from *And When You Are Young*. Reprinted by permission of the London Association for the Teaching of English.

Rex Warner: 'Mile Fishermen' from *Poems*. Reprinted by permission of The Bodley Head.

Judith Wright: 'Woman to Man' from *Collected Poems 1942–1970*. Reprinted by permission of the author and Angus & Robertson Ltd.

W. B. Yeats: 'The Wild Swans at Coole' and 'Death' from *Collected Poems*. Reprinted by permission of A. P. Watt & Son on behalf of Mr. M. B. Yeats and Macmillan, London and Basingstoke.

Yevgeney Yevtushenko: 'Waiting' and 'Schoolmaster' from *Yevtushenko: Selected Poems*, trans. Robin Milner-Gulland and Peter Levi, S.J. Translation © Robin Milner-Gulland and Peter Levi, 1972. Reprinted by permission of Penguin Books Ltd.

We are also very grateful to all the young people who have allowed us to publish their poems.

Index of first lines

◊ indicates authors still at school when the poem was written

122